Scared of the Dark

Bedtime Healing Meditation for Children

Little Blue Zen

Scared of the Dark

Copyright@ 2024 Jo Galloway

The right of the author has been asserted to her following the copyright writing, designs and patent act of Australia.

All rights reserved. No part of this book may be reproduced, stored or transmitted by any means whether auditory, graphic, mechanical, or electronic without the written permission of the author. Unauthorised reproduction of any part of this work is illegal and is punishable by law.

Unless otherwise noted, the author and the publisher make no explicit guarantees as the accuracy of the information contained in this book may differ based on individual experiences and context

ISBN: 978-1-7635801-6-9

Published by Little Blue Zen
Birdwood NSW
Printed in Australia
Cover Design: Gagan Karunchandra
Editing: Kristine Gibson
jo@littlebluezen.com
http://www.littlebluezen.com

Scared of the Dark
Bedtime Healing Meditation for Children

Jo Galloway

Your child may like other books in this series

- Bully Proof. Keeping out the bullies.

- I am Different, I am Me.

- The Magical Treasure Hunt. Building Confidence.

- The Magical Worry Balloon.

- Angelic Dreams. Meet your Guardian Angel.

- Bedwetting, Dry Nights.

- I Love School.

- A Coat of Flying Colours

INTRODUCTION

Why Healing Meditations.

As children we make sense of our experiences based on our limited understanding and perception. We may misinterpret events or draw conclusions that form the basis of limiting beliefs that influence our entire life. These beliefs become ingrained over time, shaping our thoughts, feelings and behaviours well into adulthood unless consciously challenged.

In my work as a practising Hypnotherapist, I've found that all my clients' concerns, whether rooted in fears, feelings of inadequacy, addictive behaviours, or other challenges, trace back to their early childhood experiences, interactions, and upbringing. It's important to note that these issues don't exclusively stem from abusive or dysfunctional environments; limiting beliefs can arise from various circumstances.

Parents or caregivers wield substantial influence in shaping our perceptions of ourselves and the world around us. Remarks, criticisms, or comparisons made by family members can foster beliefs about our capabilities, worthiness, or potential. Furthermore, interactions with peers, teachers, and authority figures also contribute to the formation of these beliefs. Repeated experiences of rejection or failure can solidify beliefs such as "I'm not good enough" or "I'm unworthy of love."

This realization ignited my passion for intervening at the source: working with children to prevent these beliefs from taking root and manifesting into significant challenges in adulthood. By addressing issues early on, we can guide children to develop into the best versions of themselves, free from the burden of limiting beliefs that could otherwise dominate their lives.

How Healing Meditation will help your child.

Teaching children meditation offers a multitude of benefits that can positively influence their daily lives and overall development. A regular mindfulness meditation practice provides valuable tools for managing stress, navigating emotions, and promoting overall well-being. Healing meditations, in particular, bolster your child's self-belief, helping to remove any resistance they may face in adulthood. This leads to a happier, more successful and fulfilling life.

Unlike traditional meditation, which often centres on relaxation, healing meditations go a step further by focusing on recovery, balance, and reprogramming a child's self-belief. These meditations use techniques such as breathing exercises, visualization, and guided imagery to not only foster deep relaxation but also reshape their mindset.

This targeted approach helps build a stronger sense of self-confidence and resilience. By integrating positive affirmations and emotional healing, healing meditations offer a distinct advantage over traditional methods, laying a powerful foundation for a child's future success and well-being.

Meditation can also be an effective part of your child's bedtime routine, helping to calm the mind and prepare the body for restful sleep. Techniques like guided imagery and deep breathing, as outlined in this book, can signal to the brain that it's time to wind down.

Sharing these calming moments at bedtime not only strengthens the bond between parent and child, but also creates a supportive and nurturing environment. It also sets a positive example, emphasizing the importance of self-care and mindfulness.

With patience and consistency, you can help your child develop a lifelong practice that supports their mental, emotional, and physical health. Give your child the gift of relaxation and imagination with this easy-to-read story designed to inspire and uplift.

Scared of the Dark

Join Teddy, your brave and comforting friend, on a magical bedtime journey designed to help little ones conquer their fears of the dark. In this gentle Healing Meditation, Teddy shares a heartwarming story about overcoming nighttime worries and using the power of your imagination to transform fear into bravery.

    Through soothing guidance, deep breathing and a comforting countdown, Teddy helps children relax deeply and embrace their inner courage. Ideal for easing bedtime anxieties, this meditation fosters a sense of safety and confidence, ensuring a peaceful, restful night's sleep.

In this comforting bedtime meditation, Teddy helps your child understand that their special brain can overcome fears. By gently guiding them to imagine themselves as brave and strong, Teddy encourages them to replace scary thoughts with positive ones.

As the lights go out, your child will learn to embrace the dark, thinking of all the good things in their life instead of monsters. With Teddy's support, they will feel safe, calm, and grown-up, drifting off to sleep with confidence and peace.

Delivered in a slow, monotone voice, this story captivates and soothes. Scared of the Dark, is also available on YouTube, providing a soothing auditory experience children can enjoy at home, in the car, or anywhere they need a moment of relaxation."

Listen on YouTube

6 * Scared of the Dark

Scared of the Dark

Hello, my beautiful Little Starlight.

It's time for bed.

Snuggle up with your special Teddy, because tonight Teddy has something very special to share with you.

Teddy knows you are afraid of the dark and that you feel scared when Mummy or Daddy turn off the lights.

Teddy once felt afraid of the dark too, but now he's a brave grown-up Teddy.

He's going to share a very special secret with you to help you feel brave, just like him.

Would you like that?

Before Teddy can start his story, he wants you to make yourself really comfortable.

Wriggle around a little until you find the perfect spot.

Teddy wants you to feel nice and relaxed.

Now, Teddy asks you to softly close your eyes and take a big breath in through your nose.

Hold your breath for a moment—3, 2, 1, perfect.

Now breathe out nice and slow, as if you're blowing out all your birthday candles.

That's right.

Did you notice that as you breathe deeply, your body calms down and relaxes?

Let's do that again.

Breathe in deeply, hold for 3, 2, 1… now breathe slowly out through your mouth.

Every time you breathe out, feel your body sinking down into your warm, snuggly bed.

Feel your body becoming all floppy and floaty—oh, nice and relaxed.

Teddy is breathing with you too, so just continue to breathe in and out, in and out.

Teddy says, just to be sure you're really relaxed, so you can listen closely to his story, keep taking those deep, soothing breaths.

Teddy is going to count down from 10 to 1. With each number, you'll feel yourself drifting down into a wonderful, happy place, becoming sleepier and sleepier, and more relaxed with every number he counts.

Are you ready?

10—feeling calm, warm and safe.

9—relaxing all your muscles.

8—slipping down deeper into a beautiful, relaxing spot.

7—floating down.

6—drifting down.

5—oh so sleepy… yawn.

Don't forget to breathe, says Teddy

4—feeling very comfy.

3—feeling happy.

2—feeling safe.

1—oh so peaceful.

Don't you just love bedtime?

"It's my favourite time of day," says Teddy.

You are now ready to hear my secret story.

Teddy tells you about the time when he was just a little baby teddy bear.

He used to be afraid of the dark, too.

"When the lights went out, my mind would imagine many scary monsters living under the bed or hiding behind the door," says Teddy.

I thought the dark was so scary because I couldn't see what was around me.

I imagined I could even hear the monsters, and I would shake.

My heart would pound, and my eyes were as big as saucers.

Even if I shut my eyes tight, I could still see them.

I would yell and cry for someone to turn on the lights so I could see and feel safe because my mind imagined so many scary things.

But do you know what?

The scary monsters were only in my mind, in my brain.

They weren't real at all, and not really in my room.

If I thought of a scary monster in my brain, I would see a scary monster.

My brain was that clever.

"But your brain is even better than my brain," says Teddy.

Would you like me to show you just how brilliant your special brain is?

You can keep your eyes closed, Teddy says, because you can see perfectly well with your eyes closed.

All little boys and girls have the most amazing imaginations—way better than grown-ups.

I want you to imagine you are holding a big, juicy lemon in your hand.

Bring the lemon up to your nose and smell its rich, tangy scent.

Now, put the lemon in your mouth and squeeze out all the lemony juice.

Chomp on the flesh of the lemon—chomp, chomp, chomp.

Do you notice your mouth making extra saliva or spit?

Are you wincing from the sourness?

You are telling your special brain you're eating a lemon, so your body is acting as if you can really taste that tangy lemon.

See how clever your special brain is?

You know you're not really eating a lemon, but you're telling your special brain that you are.

Now, when you go to bed at night and the lights go out, your special brain might imagine many scary monsters.

You're telling your brain you're scared and that you don't like the dark, and your body responds as if you're really, truly scared.

"But what do you think would happen, says Teddy, next time the lights go out, and you told yourself good things?"

Like how brave you are, you can talk to your special brain by saying, "I'm not afraid of the dark."

I'm brave, "I like the dark."

You can think of lots of things that are much better than scary monsters.

You could think about the wonderful day you had today, or about your friends that you like to play with.

Maybe you could imagine that special toy you want for your birthday, or the exciting things you'll do tomorrow.

You have your eyes closed so you can picture whatever you like in your special brain.

You're choosing to see good things, not monsters.

Your Mummy and Daddy are so proud of you, says Teddy.

You can tell them, "I'm not scared of the dark."

Monsters are not real.

I only imagined them in my special brain.

I'm choosing to imagine good things now.

My brilliant brain can imagine anything I want."

Teddy reminds you, "I am so brave and big now.

I have Teddy with me, and he told me that the dark changes nothing.

I can look around my room with the lights off and see that everything is still the same.

I only made up the monsters in my special brain.

See, there's nothing to fear.

There are no monsters hiding anywhere.

Your bedroom is monster-free.

You're showing your Mummy or Daddy how grown-up you are.

Being alone in your bed doesn't scare you.

I am here with you, says Teddy.

You like the dark because it is comforting and relaxing.

You love bedtime, and you are so grown-up now.

"Only babies fear the dark," says Teddy, because they don't know how to talk to their special brain.

But you're not a baby anymore.

You are big and brave.

Teddy suggests, "Let's surprise Mummy at bedtime.

When she comes in, ask her to turn off the light.

She might be a little surprised, but she'll turn off the light and close the door, leaving you and Teddy in complete darkness.

And guess what?

You're no longer afraid.

You feel happy, thinking about all the good things that happened today and the fun you're going to have tomorrow.

You're so brave and strong, and Teddy is right here with you.

You realise there's nothing to be afraid of.

The monsters are just not real—only made up on television or in stories.

You've let go of your fear.

You're all grown up now, feeling happier and calmer.

You like the dark, and you feel safe in the dark.

"There are lots of good things that happen in the dark," says Teddy

Just like the stars in the sky, you can only see them when it's dark.

And the Tooth Fairy and Santa Claus—they only visit at night, so there not afraid of the dark.

They know monsters aren't real.

The dark is the time when they like to visit all the boys and girls.

So now you know that there's nothing to be afraid of in the dark.

When you go to bed tonight, think of good things, not scary things.

You're safe, you're brave, and you're ready for sweet dreams.

You have Teddy to remind you that you are safe, you are calm, you are brave, and you are all grown up now.

You love to listen to this story every night, just to remind you of how brave and grown-up you truly are.

You know exactly how to talk to your special brain.

So, take a deep breath in, my little Starlight, and breathe out all your fears.

Say good night to Teddy, and softly allow yourself to drift peacefully off to sleep, knowing that you are very safe.

Waking up in the morning, you'll feel so proud of just how brave and grown-up you are.

Good night, my beautiful Starlight.

Sweet Dreams.........

More by Jo Galloway

Dry Nights is a captivating bedtime story crafted for children ages 3 to 7, designed to help your child wake up to a dry bed each morning. This story empowers children to reconnect their brain and their bladder, fostering better control and confidence throughout the night.

As children drift off to sleep, gentle reminders reassure them of their newfound ability to stay dry all night, no matter where they sleep. The story ends with a comforting affirmation of their success and control, ensuring that each night is a step towards waking up happy and dry.

The Magical Treasure Hunt

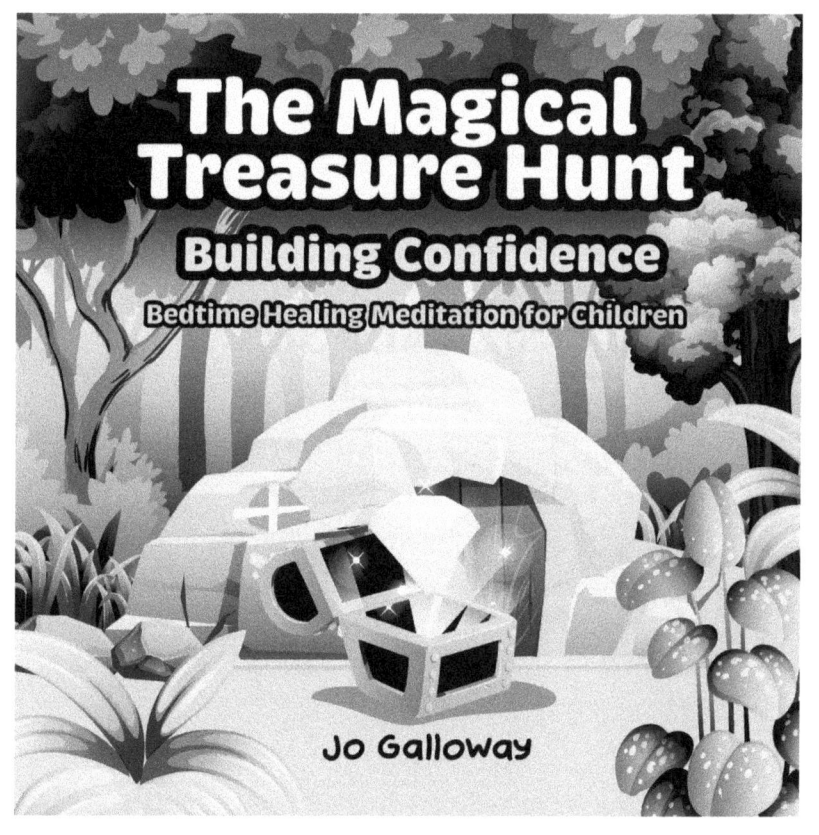

Embark on a whimsical journey with your little one as they venture into the world of self-discovery. As you guide your child through a series of relaxation exercises, they'll descend a rainbow staircase to meet their most cherished friend. Together they travel along an enchanted path. Here they'll uncover glittering stones inscribed with powerful messages: "I am lovable," "My body is beautiful just as it is," "I am good enough," and "I am confident."Each stone is a reminder of their unique strengths and worth, helping them embrace their true selves and shine with self-love and confidence.

Little Blue Zen.com

Little Blue Zen

www.ingramcontent.com/pod-product-compliance
Lightning Source LLC
Chambersburg PA
CBHW042356070526
44585CB00028B/2950